Big Book of

Kitchen Design Ideas

Schiffer Publishing Ltd

4880 Lower Valley Road, Atglen, PA 19310 USA

Big Book of

Kitchen Design Ideas

Tina Skinner

Dedication

To my father, who maintained a tradition now forgotten by far too many families—a sit-down dinner, together, every night.

Skinner, Tina.
  Big book of kitchen design ideas / Tina Skinner.
    p. cm.
  ISBN 0-7643-0672-3 (pbk.)
NK2117.K5S64   1998
747.7'97--dc21   98-23063
                                      CIP

Designed by Blair Loughrey
Type set in Korinna BT/Zapf Calligraphy

ISBN: 0-7643-0672-3
Printed in China

Published by Schiffer Publishing Ltd.
4880 Lower Valley Road
Atglen, PA 19310
Phone: (610) 593-1777; Fax: (610) 593-2002
E-mail: Schifferbk@aol.com
Please visit our web site catalog at
www.schifferbooks.com

This book may be purchased from the publisher.
Include $3.95 for shipping. Please try your bookstore first.
We are always looking for authors to write books on new and related subjects. If you have an idea for a book please contact us at the address above.
You may write for a free printed catalog.

In Europe, Schiffer books are distributed by
Bushwood Books
6 Marksbury Avenue
Kew Gardens
Surrey TW9 4JF England
Phone: 44 (0)208-392-8585; Fax: 44 (0)208-392-9876
E-mail: Bushwd@aol.com
Free postage in the UK., Europe; air mail at cost.

We are interested in hearing from authors
with book ideas on related subjects.

Contents

Introduction

The kitchen is the most important room in the house.

Few households could argue that point. The kitchen is where the day begins before family members bustle off in their multiple directions. It's where the members reconvene to discuss the day's events while savoring the day's most important meal. When friends come calling, it's where they sit down for tea, and when there's a party on, everyone invariably crams in unless doors have been closed and caterers hired to keep the kitchen clear.

The recent glut of kitchen books and magazines illustrates the increasing respect paid to this room's rank in the home, and helps chart the trend to renovate older kitchens and accentuate the room in new homes. This book takes a different approach by delivering what consumers most want—pictures. Decorating ideas are visual, and we've collected hundreds, including award winning designs and fancy product showcases designed for many of the nation's leading manufacturers of cabinetry, countertop, windows, appliances, and floors. Here is a chance to compare hundreds of paints and finishes, countertop colors, the effects of tiles, window treatments, wallpapers, stone, ...

Besides working as a library of ideas for you, this book is also intended as a tool to help a contractor or designer gauge your tastes. It is hoped that, by the time you sign on the dotted line of your credit charge at the home improvements store or on the bottom of a remodeling contract, this book will have been well used— paper clipped, book marked, and dog-eared. The manufacturers of products pictured in this book are listed in a Resource Guide at the back. They are eager to talk to consumers about the products pictured. Further, the dozens of designers, as well as designers in your own hometown, would be happy to sit and page through the pictures presented here to gauge your taste and customize the designs presented here into your lifestyle.

The National Kitchen and Bath Association will gladly recommend designers and installers in your area. The organization also offers a complete planning kit to consumers called *The What, Where, and the Who To Start Your Dream Kitchen or Bath*. That organization is listed in Resource Guide of the book, preceded by a great recommendation—thirty-nine winning designs from the NKBA's annual kitchen design competition.

Photo courtesy of DuPont Corian®

Fred and Michele Adams took an inefficient, 14 x 29 foot, U-shaped kitchen built in the 1970s and converted it using an island plan with a two-tiered center stage, handsome new cabinetry, and sleek new lighting. Corian® was used to replace the high-maintenance wood kitchen countertops and create a full-height back splash behind the range. Art Deco stencil borders and sleek lighting enhance the room's modern character.

Photo courtesy of DuPont Corian®

Photo courtesy of DuPont Corian®

Far left: A comfortable wall bench and table connect to the food preparation area of the kitchen.

Left: A desk area was incorporated in the kitchen design.

Photo courtesy of Wilsonart Laminate Flooring

Modern flooring with natural earth tones anchors this space-age kitchen firmly on the planet. Blonde Oak-colored laminate flooring by Wilsonart adds warmth to this stunning black-and-white space, perfect for a talented chef with a hungry audience.

An unusually shaped island helps create a mood of angles and planes in this modern kitchen. The countertop is Midnight and Cameo White Corian®, complementing brushed steel lighting and appliances.

This was a kitchen designed for entertaining, with a wraparound counter, a lowered bar with seating, and a serving window into the living room and focal fireplace beyond. The slick, modern design is tied together with flooring by Bruce® Hardwood Floors.

Modern materials mix with early American design for a comfortable kitchen you can work in. The laminate flooring is Plank style, Carolina Ash color by Wilsonart.

Again, creative color makes this kitchen a stand-out. Colored tile, triangles of colorful linoleum, and stenciling give this room its customized identity. White appliances, red countertop, and wood cabinetry harmonize with this unique mix of Early American and modern.

A decorative tile back splash and border treatment in the overhead light structure tie in with black appliances and Sapphire and Bone Corian® countertops. The tile design is repeated in leaded glass cabinet doors over the stove.

A sparkling clean effect from white on white is carried through in cabinets, wall color, appliances, and countertop. A wood floor and neutral rug add color and help maintain the illusion that the kitchen's owner spends every spare moment cleaning. Countertop details include a custom-routed drain board and Sapphire inlay for a spark of color.

Light blues and grays give this room an eternal twilight feeling. A traditional layout of wrap counter and adjacent family seating area are tied together by Congoleum Evolution® "Gemstone" luxury tile.

An exotic, Japanese flair was achieved in this intimate seating area, with designer chairs matching wall hangings, and lighting. Black and green cabinets and walls hold their own with glass block wall and Evolution® "Diamond Quartz" Luxury Tile by Congoleum.

Photos Courtesy of Bomanite® Corp.

A modern kitchen with all the flair of a fancy restaurant, with sculpted ceiling, stainless steel appliances, and a seated bar suitable for the best of culinary shows. One of the most elegant touches in this kitchen is right under your feet—the Patène Artectura floor by Bomanite, a customized concrete system that utilizes a variety of coloring, texturing, and finishing methods.

A colorful rug on beech flooring creates a centerpiece for this unique dining table. The kitchen work areas are de-emphasized, set against one wall in a solid, neutral color to allow the table, stairs, and an adjacent art work to stand out.

Photo courtesy of The Hardwood Council

Cabinets are a crucial kitchen component, both for function and design. These custom-built cabinets by The Kennebec Company, along with a high-gloss wood floor and window trim, turn this kitchen into a showplace.

Photo courtesy of The Kennebec Company

A curved counter and seating area mates with arched doorway and
draws the kitchen out into the larger living and dining areas beyond.

Design and function are married in a smart, modern design with
frameless blue cabinetry and appliance panels, a coordinating cutout
design in the flooring, and bold, brick-red accents. Dual islands allow for
seating and multiple cooks. The cleaning area is kept separate from the
stove and a separate sink helps to accommodate multiple occupants.

Above: Double sinks on a kitchen island allow guests to remain seated, out of the cook's way, while they fix a drink. Covers on the sink expand the space. A unique design element here is the way semi-circular seats mirror the island sinks and hanging lamps above.

Left: An unconventional kitchen color works nicely here, paired with black countertop, a light stain on the cabinets, and inset glass blocks that filter in outdoor light.

Photo courtesy of Pergo

Here is a sleek slash of kitchen, modern and utilitarian with a stretch of counter and cooktop, a wall of storage. The focus in this narrow world is on food, with a social gathering spot at the opening in an extension of counter complete with seats.

Above & Opposite: This sociable kitchen by designer Johnny Grey was conceived of as a place for people to congregate and entertain comfortably and efficiently. Varied countertop heights and a central island are predominate features. Unconventional, custom cabinetry and a Jenn-Air dishwasher and double oven combine to create an efficient cooking area. Clean dishes stack above the dishwasher. Lacking the traditional window over the kitchen sink, shelves and adornments add interest to a brightly painted wall. A sitting area, complete with couch and dining table (not shown) adjoin the cooking area.

Stainless steel is the hot, industrial in-home look. "Stainless-steel appliances have increased in popularity because the finish works well with so many different kitchen styles," says Johnna Rogers, a certified kitchen designer and owner of The Keeping Room design business in Zionsville, Ind. "The clean, sleek style of stainless steel not only complements the decor of most kitchens, but it is durable and timeless."

An island creates seating and additional workspace for the cook. Oak cabinetry and flooring make this kitchen timeless.

Distinct work stations create zones in this kitchen design by Jean Cain, with an enormous island tying kitchen and living areas together. Exposed, painted beams magnify the space, and cherry flooring anchors and unites the diverse elements.

This kitchen is stunning in its individual accents of quality, charming in their blend. Colorful windowpanes, unique tile borders under the window and around the in-wall fireplace, and the checked green-and-white island countertop lend character to the room. Painted beams and an old-fashioned sink help complete the air of simple charm.

Two handsome, semi-circle serving cherry bars and end cabinets provide a grand entrance to this kitchen.

A rounded counter extension adds workspace and helps connect this small kitchen to other rooms. A rich walnut floor ties dining area to kitchen, and contrasts beautifully with red oak cabinetry.

Photo courtesy of Kohler Co.

Photo courtesy of Southern Pine Council

Above: This stunning kitchen requires a nearby pantry to stash all the stuff. But what a worthwhile sacrifice. The walls here have been reserved for displaying china and an assortment of bottles and containers.

Left: A small island allows for seating and increases the food preparation area in this small kitchen. A Southern pine beaded ceiling, floor, and countertop help divide the room into upper and lower zones and provide visual relief from large expanses of white.

New York designer James Wood had two zones in mind, separated by an island, when he put together this Performance by Design Kitchen: a food preparation zone against the far wall and the island and foreground area for eating, socializing, and using the cookbooks, recipe box, and computer. Splashes of pure color are provided by the Blue Creek™ appliances by Jenn-Air. Natural light is amply supplied by a sidewall of floor-to-ceiling opaque glass. The back wall is sheathed in square gray, hand-cut Ann Sacks glass tiles arranged in a subtle plaid, with alternating sandblasted and polished tiles to enhance their reflective qualities. The countertops are two pale tones of Formica Corporation's Surell, and the floor is covered with wide, seamless sheets of Armstrong's new Vios, which has the look of embossed leather.

Far left: A 20-cubic-foot side-by-side refrigerator and double electric wall oven from Blue Creek™ by Jenn-Air in Jade Green.

Left: Here Jenn-Air transforms the normally utilitarian dishwasher into a kitchen ornament with their Bordeaux Red Ultimate Quiet Dishwasher.

An incredible amount of storage space was created in this kitchen by custom cabinet builders Rutt. The basic style is Yorkshire, kept neutral by Toffee Paint contrasted with turquoise-color tile back splashes.

2 Country

One of the most enduring styles, country design is dominant in the United States market. Incorporating oodles of charm, from farm animal ornaments to antique plates and crockery, country encompasses lots of design elements. Textiles that complement the style range from ruffled floral prints to gay ginghams and plaids. Any number of natural elements can be worked in, from wicker to ceramics, cast-iron to copper. Country works well with natural wood cabinets, or any number of basic colors, from stark white to warm greens and reds.

Photo courtesy of IXL Cabinets

A bold floral wallpaper, black china, and black appliances make a bold statement in this kitchen, contrasting with exposed beams, wood-grain laminate flooring, and natural wood Branford™ cabinets.

Above: Modern and brand spanking new, this kitchen was designed with classic country characteristics like natural wood stain cabinets and open beams, combined with modern conveniences like a big-pane picture window and easy-maintenance, manufactured flooring.

Left: Country charm is evoked in blue and white fabrics and wall borders set against the Liberty Oak Square cabinets by Wellborn. A corner sink base cabinet and a microwave cabinet give the kitchen more usable countertop space in addition to a unique design.

Ceramic floor tiles key in with countertop and back splash for a rich, classic look. Basket drawers in the island are a nice, country touch.

Photo courtesy of IXL Cabinets

Photo courtesy of Wellborn Cabinet, Inc.

Above: Lines and angles, enhanced by the wallpaper and a unique window, are key design elements here. The island, likewise, takes some interesting twists, with a slate-blue countertop and Tiara™ cabinet design in maple to mimic the walls beyond.

Left: A Colonial-style kitchen features distinctive design ideas such as the tambour unit area with cassette drawer units, a fret valance, and open shelf areas. The cabinets are in the WellBuilt Select door style in oak, with a light oak stain.

Left: A blue wash on white cabinets gives this kitchen a bright, airy look, balanced by a "wood" floor of Congoleum Forum® Plank Quiet Laminate flooring. A handy desk doubles as extra counter space and seating for a guest in this small work space.

Below: Colorful tiles characterize this kitchen, as back splash to sink, ornament above stove, and on the island countertop. These are offset by neutral tones in the cabinets and sponge-painted walls and the muted Futura® "Casa Grande" resilient sheet flooring by Congoleum.

Photos courtesy of Congoleum

Photos courtesy of DuPont Corian®

Above & Left: In the landmark Latshaw mansion in Kansas City, Missouri, a turn-of-the century kitchen was transformed by designer Kristeen Armstrong-Scott, CKD, of Armstrong Kitchens. In the main kitchen, Corian® countertops of Aurora are complemented by back splashes of Bone, overlaid with Aurora. These surfaces alone did wonders in terms of bringing the kitchen up to date. In the adjoining butler's pantry, a "tablecloth edge" was sculpted in Summit Pyrenees to create a unique focal point.

Left: Decorative wall and floor tiles adorn this kitchen nook. The square floor pattern is repeated above the top cabinets. Tile is also used to create a durable work area for food preparation.

Below: Stone and tile combine to make the stove the focal point of this open, inviting kitchen, along with a duo-height island for seating, eating, and working. The scene is underlined by Forum® Plank "Colonial Cherry" Quiet Laminate flooring by Congoleum.

White appliances and countertops blend for a clean kitchen corner, framed by a light floral wallpaper and windowpane check linoleum floor. Black countertops add contrast and interest, forming a focal point at the island where a white range sets the stage for entertaining.

A busy feeling is created in this room, with check floor, colorful wallpaper and ceiling border, and leaded windowpanes. A handsome match was achieved in the cabinet stain and Evolution® "Plaza Court" Luxury Tile border design by Congoleum.

A high ceiling allows for a second story of upper cabinets in the Hampton™ Arched style, with beautiful antique-glass windows to provide light and openness.

A pantry corner with all the charm of a mountain cabin, this cabinetry was fashioned from oak and enhanced with a custom finish called Chocolate Frosting. The cabinet on the right has glazed chicken wire panels on top, and display windows in the grain bin drawers.

Countertop wraps around the cook, providing easy access to workspace and creating a cozy nook for culinary creation. The dark countertop, border-strip paper, and accent china contrast with white Quadric™ cabinets.

Right: A playful, green and white theme tops wood tones including Regal Plank™ "Royal Cherry" Quiet Laminate flooring by Congoleum.

Photo courtesy of Congoleum

Below: Matching panels over modern appliances maintain the English country manor atmosphere in this kitchen. The rich effect is carried through with tile countertops and a luminous wood floor.

Photos courtesy of Whirlpool®
Home Appliances

Photo courtesy of IXL Cabinets

Swinging French doors and slatted window shutters are unique architectural details in this kitchen. Another handy element is the two-level island packed with storage space in a cabinet design—Hampton™—that matches those on the walls.

Left: Natural, stained panel board and the ceramic look of Light Kraft/Ash Rose colored Highlight® "Modern Mosaic" resilient sheet flooring from Congoleum combine for an outdoorsy, country feeling indoors. Blue countertop, curtains, and accents add charm to the straightforward character of this kitchen design.

Below: White cabinets make a statement against natural browns and greens in this spacious kitchen design. The frameless cabinets are the Cambria Square Ivory Chiffon model from Wellborn. The side hutch with stacked cabinets offers a furniture look, as does the multi-level island.

Photo courtesy of Congoleum

Photo courtesy of Wellborn Cabinet, Inc.

The Light Pewter/Bluestone color of this Congoleum Ova-tions® resilient sheet flooring ties kitchen and sitting room together. The neutral pattern, "Buckingham," creates texture, blending with polka-dot wallpaper for a fresh, country feel.

The appeal of wood flooring is an enduring one, which is fortunate, since the real thing lasts a long time. Here, Southern pine flooring fits in with a modern look created with white cabinetry.

Faux marble flooring dominates this room setting, picked up by green accents in the cabinets and a ceiling border. The resilient sheet flooring is Futura® "Roman Elegance" in Midnight Green by Congoleum.

This kitchen island doubles as a dining table and extra counter space. Don't let the country charm of all that wood fool you, the professional oven and range were installed for a serious cook.

Wood details were added to this room using a simple system of wood planks and battens connected with aluminum clips, called Natural Impressions™ invented by HDM USA. The ceiling planks and molding add character and architecture to this kitchen.

Alternating blocks of black set the boundaries in this off-white kitchen space. Kitchen, brick wall, and cabinets blend together in one seamless color, allowing adornments like the crockery and plate collections to really stand out.

Photo courtesy of The Kennebec Company

Here black appliances contrast with wood cabinetry and flooring—a blend of modern and early American.

Finishing touches, such as the molding stained to match the cabinets, and the hand-painted grapevines, make this kitchen unique. Wood panels on the refrigerator were also stained to match the custom cabinetry.

Photo courtesy of Sherwin-Williams

Two tone cabinets, with lots of little details like the plate rack and spice drawers, lend this kitchen its allure.

A checkerboard floor and matching tiles on the sink back splash tie this kitchen together. The cabinets are Westmere style by Merillat.

Counter space as far as the eye can see! This spacious kitchen is a cook's dream, with plenty of room for preparing food and displaying kitchen collectibles. Because there was so much room for display, plenty of shelves and open spaces were provided in the Pennington-style oak cabinets by Yorktowne.

Wood colors and textures dominate this kitchen, with dark beams, cherry cabinetry, and an oak floor. The open roof and beams create an incredible, lofty feel to this kitchen and dining space. The food preparation area has been carefully sectioned off from the great room with counters that make it easy for people to cozy up for conversation while staying out of the cook's way.

Photos courtesy of The Hardwood Council

This set of hickory cabinets by Wellborn allows plenty of space for display, from the plate rack above, to a fancy cut-out corner floor cabinet for the fancy tureens.

A window seat is a welcome component in a kitchen—a center of comfort in the heart of the home. Here those waiting to eat can watch the cook at work, and afterward the cook can laze while others clean up. There is a natural finish on the Avondale-style cabinetry by Yorktowne Cabinets, which includes a plate rack and decorative under-counter storage.

A wonderful, light and airy feeling is created with creams and light blue accents in vertical-stripe curtains and diamond Designer Inlaid™ "Trellis" resilient sheet flooring by Congoleum.

Photo courtesy of Yorktowne® Cabinets

Photo courtesy of DuPont Corian®

Above: Simplicity and utility combine for an attractive, economical kitchen. The doors and drawers of Yorktowne's Medford-style cabinets are handle free, so there are no distractions from the clean, simple lines. The cabinets are Autumn Laminate.

Left: An expanse of Blue Ridge Corian® with Bisque edge treatment maximized the usefulness of this small kitchen area.

Left & below: Hardwood flooring is used to artistically divide up zones in this kitchen dining area.

Wood takes center stage in this kitchen, with gorgeous flooring and trim complementing light and dark finishes on the cabinetry.

Photo courtesy of Rutt Custom Cabinetry

Cabinetry details embellish this beautifully furnished kitchen. Open plate and cup racks, a decorative shelf above the stove, and an open island filter light from nearby windows throughout this semi-enclosed space. Custom built by Rutt Cabinetry in English Manor style with toffee paint.

Dark cabinets create a rich, regal effect, complemented by Designer Inlaid™ "Bouquet" resilient sheet flooring in Wine/Wheat by Congoleum.

A column and classic detailing lend a Roman look to this kitchen. The Empire-style cabinets were stained mahogany cherry by custom craftsmen to blend with the marble countertop and walls and a polished stone floor.

A warm, hand-wiped stain reveals the smooth beauty of maple cabinetry. Each Cameo style door has beaded lip detailing on overlay doors. A matching dishwasher panel integrates the appliance, creating a sleek baseline. Black countertop also ties in with the appliances.

Photo courtesy of Plain & Fancy Custom Cabinetry

Photos courtesy of DuPont Corian®

Left & above: Solid lines give this kitchen its classic look, in the wallpaper, in the cabinets, and in the edge treatment on the Corian® countertops. The pattern is carried through in the double sink of Corian®.

Photos courtesy of DuPont Corian®

Designer Sarah L. Reep used handsome topped tile and Cameo White Corian® on the work areas, along with custom-built cabinets by Fieldstone Cabinetry, inc. that incorporate molding for a classic look.

Photo courtesy of Andersen Windows, Inc.

Whatever else you use in the rest of your house, designers at Andersen Windows advise that you seriously consider what kind of window you install over your kitchen sink. No one wants to climb onto a large, wet sink to push up or pull down a double-hung window. Here, an Andersen gliding window requires only a horizontal push to open or close.

Bold wallpaper frames custom-built arched windows. The cabinets, tile countertops, and back splashes around the periphery are white, while red tile on the island ties in to the wallpaper.

Wood and brick team up for a fantastic effect in this high-ceilinged kitchen design. The cabinetry is Hancock Natural by Wellborn with a natural finish on hickory wood. The kitchen design incorporates a wheeled island, useful for work, serving, and tucking away when not in use.

Photo courtesy of Wellborn Cabinet, Inc.

Here's a kitchen anyone would covet. Designer Beverly Ellsley had an enormous space to work with, and made it all intimate with nooks and unique features like the semi-circular seating area tucked in the central area. She incorporated a little work desk, a mishmash of maple cabinetry, and lots of windows to add interest at every angle. One unique feature is a cutout to the second floor, complete with lathed railing used to dry flowers and herbs.

Photo courtesy of Thermador

Sleek stainless steel appliances lend this kitchen its professional utility, including a 45-inch steel gas cooktop and a 36-inch professional range.

A glass chandelier, a Roman column, and an Oriental carpet lend classic touches to this modern kitchen, complete with industrial-strength, stainless steel appliances from the Pro-Style™ line of commercial-style appliances by Jenn-Air.

Scene-enhancing details in this kitchen include decorative tile inserts and antiquing on the cabinets.

Photos courtesy of Wellborn Cabinet, Inc.

Elegance lies in the custom cherry woodworking details in this kitchen cabinetry by Wellborn Cabinet, Inc. A two-level island includes spice drawers and display windows. Silver drawers and a plate rack are framed within a columned architectural addition, tied in with the rest of the room via heavy molding and a bold stripe.

Photo courtesy of IXL Cabinets

Tudor™ Arched cabinets, a reproduction beer sign and
antique china give this kitchen its period flare. One attraction
is a lighted display case for prized crystal and china pieces.

Painted cabinetry lends an Early American feel to this room, and provides a neutral color against which a collection of kitchen antiques is displayed. Note how the top cabinets and shelves slant back toward the ceiling, opening up the room and providing the majority of storage on the more accessible lower shelves. A wide-plank wood floor completes the effect.

Photos courtesy of DuPont Corian®

Tile inlay and fanciful molding in this bisque countertop and on the range hood add character to a white kitchen setting. The corner range hood is the centerpiece, with a stenciled grapevine, a tile backdrop, and some beautiful copper pots displayed below. The white cabinetry and clean lines lend a modern touch to this period theme.

Photos courtesy of Elmira Stove Works

One of the hardest things about making a country, Victorian, or log home kitchen look old is having to install new appliances. That's why Elmira Stove Works started making an antique-styled appliance line more than twenty years ago, with ranges, convection wall ovens, microwaves, refrigerators, and panel kits for refrigerators and dishwashers.

Craftsmanship recreates the understated beauty of early American kitchens, along with a reproduction oven and range. An island piece can be moved for convenience.

Ash cabinetry and matching beams in a picture window give this room its custom-designed grace. It was designed for a cook, with a large, open range and an enormous island dedicated solely to chopping and other food-related chores.

Cherry cabinetry, paneling, and moldings by Wood-Mode break up two distinct patterns—square tiles and stylized wallpaper. A big window completes the picture.

A metal wall, with wooden horse sculptures, lends character to this kitchen, complementing an old-fashioned stainless steel sink and classic cabinetry.

Chairs, door and window frames tie in color to this gorgeous wood and white kitchen setting. Cabinetry dominates the walls in this small work space, but the addition of an island adds an expanse of countertop work surface.

Tall cabinetry helps compensate for lack of space in this narrow kitchen. A rug and the direction of the floorboards helps make the space appear larger.

Photos courtesy of The Kennebec Company

An heirloom china set gets a frame.

Above & Opposite: In a celebration of America's design heritage, this kitchen also combines the amenities of modern living. Various cabinet styles and paneling by Wood-Mode, as well as adapted antiques, further the illusion of an 18th-century keeping room. The two-tier, L-shaped island defines sitting and home office area. Track lighting mounted on painted beams and an iron chandelier illustrate modern and antique lighting options. Twin 30-inch ranges from Jenn-Air are backlit by a copper-laminate back splash. The upper cabinets are painted black over a red finish to give the illusion of age. The mariner's compass on the range hood is Crossville Ceramics tile.

Antique green cabinets and hand-painted walls work well to soften the effect of white appliances and countertop.

Left: White acts as background in this kitchen design, allowing subtle details to really jump out, like the wrought-iron candelabra and chairs, the open shelves with arched top, the tan tiles in the white back splash, and the raw wood beams.

Below: The grays of a stone sink and counter and pewter collectibles are framed by custom cabinetry in this early American kitchen setting.

Photos courtesy of The Kennebec Company

Exposed beams, a dark finish, and light filtered through clouded glass give this kitchen its Early American atmosphere.

An enormously attractive corner—custom cabinets vary in size, lending interest to this expanse of wood, complemented by black countertop and a brick floor with Oriental carpet.

A section of tree, finished with the bark still attached, makes a unique table and centerpiece for this log cabin. Rough-hewn, natural finished cabinets, along with a collection of wooden birdhouses and antique crockery help maintain the charm. But, of course, it is a modern kitchen, with electricity. So, to be as unobtrusive as possible, yet without apologizing for their presence, black appliances and a Black Black sink by Kohler were incorporated.

Rustic, Early American charm was achieved by designer Barbara Hauben-Ross using a simple hanging frame and a primitive island of cherry.

Decorative cutouts in these wall cabinets put them on center stage in this custom-designed kitchen. The entire kitchen benefits from custom cabinetry, including the refrigerator, dishwasher and stove, with wood panels. The expansive island has a place to tuck away stools, and to tuck legs under when seated. Exposed wood beams create contrast with the hand-finished cabinets and wide-plank floor.

Photos courtesy of The Kennebec Company

Gray countertop gets double treatment, above and below the island, with lathed legs to make this a stand-out in the ever-popular island kitchen design department. A natural finish on the maple cabinetry complements the gray.

Photos courtesy of The Kennebec Company

Left: There are a number of reasons to vary counter height. Besides visual interest, a lowered counter is more accessible for children and physically challenged adults. Also, some chores are easier on a lower counter, such as kneading dough.

Below: A variety of textures lend country charm to this kitchen setting. There is painted paneling around a brick fireplace, an arched brick doorway over stone flooring, finished wood beams contrasted with wicker baskets and copper pots, and a rough-woven rug over wide-plank wood flooring.

5 | **Retro and Art Deco**

Nostalgia in the home decorating field doesn't always extend all the way back to the days of yore. In fact, fads from our recent past are being revived as people seek to recreate memories from times they themselves can actually remember. Popular periods include the *Happy Days* of the 1950s, the hot colors of the 1960s and '70s, and an increasing interest in a time our grandparents may reminisce about—the Roaring Twenties.

Photo courtesy of Kohler Co.

Here's a bold kitchen design, with red cabinets contrasted with white appliances and countertop, and a black sink for good measure. Built for the convenience connoisseur, this kitchen wasted little space on countertop, opting to put the refrigerator and microwave within easy access. The effect is early '70s mod.

Photo courtesy of Rutt Custom Cabinetry

Art Deco styling and incredible craftsmanship give this kitchen all it needs in terms of decoration. Stainless steel appliances and a faux granite countertop add practicality and utility.

Bright, clean tile dominates this room. The blue theme is carried through in the cabinet handles, countertop, and decorative floor.

Photo courtesy of Crossville Porcelain Stone

The timeless look of wood flooring might fool you—this is actually Quiet Laminate flooring by Congoleum, chestnut-colored Forum® Plank. Green cabinets and yellow walls subtly recreate the late 1960s, for a mellow retro feel.

Photo courtesy of Congoleum

Casement windows with exclusive Andersen Art Glass®, along with custom cabinetry, make this kitchen a show stopper. Two tones of wood create a geometric, Art Deco look for this comfy kitchen setting, tying in with window trim and flooring. The built-in bench seat and kitchen table make it easy to sit and enjoy the view, too.

A distinctly different feeling is created
when the windowpanes of the previous
kitchen are replaced with plate glass.

Usurping Small Spaces

Photo courtesy of DuPont Corian®

Natural wood and white abut in this small, efficient kitchen. A decorative, full-height back splash wash was created using Glacier White Corian® routed to look like tile with Magna Sahara inlay to match the countertop.

Flair is added to this basic kitchen design by picking up colors from the floor and mimicking it in the edge treatment on a countertop of Corian®.

Photo courtesy of DuPont Corian®

Photos courtesy of DuPont Corian®

Above & Left: An awkward space is fully utilized here, tying together two separate areas of the home and extending the kitchen. The design encompasses a casual, benched seating area, a desk area for writing recipes, or preparing them, great stretches of counter space, and lots of windows to the outdoors.

Designer Greg Peacock used a tile back splash and custom cabinetry to give this small kitchen a classic look. By concentrating the cooking and cleaning areas, he left broad expanses of countertop for working and displays. An attached eating and serving counter reverses the two-tone colors of the Corian® countertops.

Photos courtesy of DuPont Corian®

The working area in this kitchen is minimal, but the utility is maximized. Cabinetry dominates one wall and additional storage is located under the island. The sink and dishwasher are located closest to thirsty guests and dirty dishes, and a tidy black tile back splash above Cameo White Corian® countertop defines the cook's workspace. Most importantly, space is reserved for big doors leading out to a stone patio area and garden.

This kitchen also serves as a passageway from one end of the home to another. In order to make passersby as unobtrusive as possible, a pathway was left, complete with the most common stop—the refrigerator—while the main cooking and cleaning areas were separated for the cook's convenience.

Tuck-away features help utilize a small kitchen space. Pull-out islands act as seating and additional workspace, storing neatly away under the oven. Also, two trays pull out and create a place for baby to sit and eat while a parent works at the counter.

A wide hallway becomes a pantry with this beautiful custom cabinet.

Photos courtesy of IXL Cabinets

Tudor™ cabinets carry through food preparation to dining areas, unifying two rooms. A service counter and china cabinet create storage space, and expansive counters allow for display and expanded work area.

Unique grain characteristics and raised-panel door styling distinguish Coronet™ cabinets in solid plantation hardwood.

A double-line of Bisque inlay on this Blue Ridge Corian® countertop creates interest and detail. A coved back splash helps with cleanup.

A custom-designed wall cabinet in the Cherry Hill Cathedral style from Wellborn has detailed door and drawer panels and a three-step door and drawer-edge perimeter.

A special entertainment center has been set aside in this kitchen, with a built-in wine rack and a sink dedicated to serving beverages. the kitchen is unified by Aspen™ style cabinets in maple.

An alcove for entertaining, with a wet bar and food prep area extend the kitchen into the dining room in this house. The two are tied together by a distinctive laminate flooring— Copperstone Tile by Wilsonart.

Multi Tasking

Photo courtesy of IXL Cabinets

The natural beauty of wood and the easy-care attributes of laminate are combined with square, flat white panel doors with contrasting edge banding crowned with solid wood pulls in the Eclipse™ cabinet design. This kitchen is set up for cooking and hanging out, in addition to daily bookkeeping chores, homework, etc.

For the busy parent, this kitchen design allows all manner of chores to be completed—cooking, laundry, and bills—while the little ones are never out of sight. All of the appliances are located on the periphery, allowing play room. And when mom or dad are ready to relax, they can simply retire to chairs at the other side.

Why lug dirty dishes all the way back from the table to the cooking area when you can stop at an island? This dishwasher is strategically placed to keep the cooking and cleaning areas separate. An adjacent laundry room makes it easier to keep two tasks going.

Photo courtesy of IXL Cabinets

This kitchen is cozy, yet incorporates many of the design elements demanded by today's homeowners—a desk work area, and an island for increased countertop workspace. Cabinets fully utilize the room to maximize storage. The Tiara™ Arched cabinets mimic the arched window and rounded island end to unify the kitchen's style.

Every kitchen has a junk drawer and a place where papers are piled up. Therefore, contemporary kitchen designs often include a desk area, here complete with matching cabinetry. Besides the junk drawers, this office space includes decorative and handy letter bins. Below, the laurel strip floor is by Bruce© Hardwood Floors.

100

Photos courtesy of Whirlpool® Home Appliances

In a home designed to be "less challenging," countertops are only 30 inches off the ground and nothing blocks the vision of a wheelchair-bound person. A dark border on the floor warns someone with low vision that there is a solid surface ahead. Work stations are organized to make tasks less challenging—a second sink is placed near the lowered stove. Controls are in front to aid access. Leg room is left under counters to assist people in wheelchairs as they cook, wash dishes, or remove items from the refrigerator.

Hints and plans for "less challenging" kitchens are available by writing to Whirlpool® Home Appliances at the address listed in the "Resource" section of this book.

Creative coloring serves another purpose besides decorating here. The bright stripes on contrasting colors of countertops and floor borders serve as a warning and guide to the visually impaired.

Called the Timesmart kitchen by Whirlpool®, this kitchen is the perfect spot for entertaining, or for a busy family attempting to get the work done. A two-tiered counter allows for comfortable seating, complete with leg room. On the other side, the chef has room to wash, chop, and simmer. All of the appliances are within easy reach. Double sinks and microwaves allow competing chefs space to go their separate ways. The raised dishwasher increases accessibility, especially for seniors, pregnant women, people confined to wheelchairs, or those with bad backs.

Wood and white contrast in this cozy kitchen and dining area. Don't let the flooring fool you, though, it's actually easy maintenance laminate flooring by Wilsonart, Plank style in Revival Oak color—an attractive option for a family expecting lots of future spills.

Photo courtesy of Wilsonart Laminate Flooring

Recognizing that a family spends most of its time in the kitchen, this home was equipped for a lot of floor wear. Here two styles of laminate flooring create a transition between a slightly elevated kitchen and dining area—Northern Birch Plank style and Verdi Fossil Tile.

Photos courtesy of Whirlpool® Home Appliances

Appliance arrangement is a matter of personal taste and convenience. For the frequent fryer, the stove is right in the middle of the room, with a pop-up air vent. A baker, on the other hand, might prefer that big expanse of counter unfettered by a range. Likewise, the side-by-side or double-door refrigerator is a perfect pairing with the island range, allowing one to snack while another stirs the pot. A full door is more appropriate when there is no one about to be knocked into the stew.

Maximum Exposure

Left: Black appliances, wood cabinetry, and faux marble countertop combine for this beach-front kitchen. The low counter and sink area, and a sunken dining area assure that the view is never obstructed.

Below: Matching panels blend dishwasher, compactor, and refrigerator with the cabinetry in this sunny, high-ceilinged kitchen. Seating areas at the cooking island are strategically placed so that everyone can enjoy the window view.

Photos courtesy of Whirlpool® Home Appliances

Above: White, and lots of it, work with green and lavender accents for a bright kitchen done in the English Manor style by Rutt Custom Cabinetry.

Left: Two arched windows are the focal points in this room. The window over the sink is framed by corner-shelves in the simple, functional Gemini™ cabinet design.

Left: Neutral flooring and walls act as frame to wood cabinets and add a European flair to this simple, open-kitchen design. The laminate flooring is Capisto Sand by Wilsonart.

Below: An enormous island doubles both work and storage space in this kitchen. The cabinet design is Shasta™ by IXL Cabinets, a division of Triangle Pacific Corp., with flat-panel laminate doors.

A feature window combination, showcased by the arch Flexiframe window, floods this gorgeous kitchen with light. The island's rounded stone countertop, custom-made wood cabinets, and high ceiling all continue the arched theme.

This kitchen is all openness and light, with glass-fronted cabinets along the stove wall—accented by an Andersen circle window—and a southern exposure to the sun with venting and non-venting roof windows and casement windows above the sink.

Arched windows, gray walls, and white cabinets and counters give this Aspen kitchen its character.

Base cabinets painted American Tavern Green balance a generous helping of window, made more dramatic by vertically striped
wallpaper. Oak trim finishes off the custom job by Rutt Cabinetry.

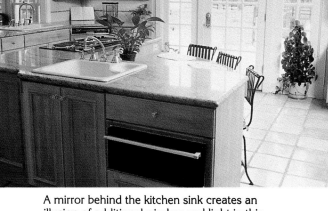

A mirror behind the kitchen sink creates an
illusion of additional window and light in this
design by Pamela Brunderman. Above, carved
relief work on the maple cabinetry adds elegance.

The beauty of wood is all the decoration this
kitchen needs. White walls, fixtures, and appliances
merely help the custom cabinetry stand out. Red
flooring and countertop tie the room together.

The photos in this chapter are all of winning designs from an annual design competition sponsored by the National Kitchen & Bath Association. They represent the best efforts of designers in meeting a variety of needs ranging from small apartments and condos to luxury kitchens in spacious homes.

Photo by Northlight Photography/Courtesy of NKBA

A river view is maximized in a small kitchen and used as the primary decoration for this sunny kitchen designed by Dena Rae Jurries of Boise, Idaho. Clean black and white cabinets, floor, and countertop allow blue water and sky to shine to their maximum, with a little red accent on the bench chairs and towel. To make up for space lost to window, an island becomes both storage cabinet, table, and handy countertop.

Photos courtesy of NKBA

Above: Traffic flow is managed and counter space maximized with this attached work area. Designer Susan M. Larsen used neutral colors in cabinets, floors, and tile countertop so that the special little details, like the rabbit planter and the floral ceiling border, really stand out.

Left: An arch ties kitchen to living areas of the home in this design by Diane H. Small. High cabinets over the stove maximize storage space. Highlight tiles add color, along with a bright painting.

A ceiling light mimics the shape of the check-shaped island below in this design by Jack L. Busby. A modern effect is created with dark appliances, black floor and molding, and smoked-glass cabinet doors. Lighting over the counters and spot lighting keep the work spaces well lit.

An enormous island with brass rail graces this spacious, enviable kitchen, complete with eight-burner stove and acres of counter space—perfect for the frequent entertainer. Designer Martha Sasso and S. J. Pappas magnified the spacious effect further with white cabinets and panels for dishwasher and refrigerator appliances. Wood flooring and an antique runner provide warmth and make it easier to maintain the appearance of spotlessness.

This kitchen was designed for cooking. Designer Robert Wieland underwrote the sleek efficiency of this space in black and white, with lines that curve and stretch. Chrome trim ties in cabinets and compliments the white/gray theme.

This kitchen was designed for cooking. With the knowledge that nobody ever leaves the kitchen anyway, designer Robert Wieland made an island for them out of chef's way, with easy access to an under-counter wine and beverage cooler and a smoked glass bar. The TV is at hand, too, in case the football game is underway while the munchies are still in the oven.

114

Black and white create contrast in this sleek, modern kitchen designed by Joyce Bishop.

Rich earth tones give a warm, stately feel to this U-shaped kitchen designed by Gary S. Johnson. Faux marble back splash and window trim complements the Oriental carpet on the floor. Light is funneled in via skylight and window, and magnified by creamy countertop.

An extra sink on this granite-topped island makes entertaining easier in a spacious kitchen design by Candace Ihlenfeldt.

The versatility of black and white are explored here by designer Jason Landau. A granite back splash and sponge-painted walls mute the dramatic effects of handle-less cabinets and glossy black countertop. Designed for serious entertainers, the kitchen incorporates two range-top ovens with a griddle. A seating area and the refrigerator were placed outside the cooking area to reduce traffic around the chef.

117

Designer Merrie Fredericks used black for the appliances to downplay them in this nature-based kitchen of wood, brick-colored tiles, and granite countertops.

118

Double islands allow for seating and additional workspace. Highlights of this design by Molly J. Korb include a brass hood over the stove, arched windows, and a unique column effect in the curved seating island.

A small kitchen becomes a showplace in this design by Annette M. DePaepe. A brushed steel range hood and copper pots provide metallic accents to wood and white space. A shelf above the cabinets defines the generous ceiling height.

Designer Maureen O'Brien-Morsch created a classic Americana look, combining cast iron, stainless steel stove, and copper range hood and display. Granite countertop and stone tile with an inset square for the table complete the aura of quality.

A remarkable kitchen, designer Joan DesCombes packed this space with texture, from the tin ceiling to the multi-toned tile floor. A bold granite countertop and back splash set off a classic porcelain sink. Solid wood cabinets with a natural finish mate with an island, and delicate curtains define the spacious windows.

An unusual space is defined in this design by Delores L. Hyden. An office space now connects bookkeeper to cook to diners for the multiple chores required of kitchens.

Above: Designer Karen Richmond let the sun shine in this airy design. And when the sun isn't out, spotlights and recessed track lights illuminate this space. Glass-front cabinets take an appropriately high position in the design, along with an open-check floor pattern.

Right: Wood and tile define work and recreation areas in this kitchen. Designer touches by Daniel J. Lenner include alternating tiles on the back splash and relief molding above the cabinet-covered refrigerator.

A black countertop, floor, and ceiling band frame nat
tones in this modern kitchen designed by Karen Edw

An industrial look is created in this unique kitchen by designers Kelly L. Peterson and Catherine A. Dulacki. Cast cement column and ceiling, along with exposed pipes and dramatic spotlights set the stage for this kitchen, and a stainless steel backdrop behind the food preparation areas completes the scene.

Photo by David Livingston/Courtesy of NKBA

A mirror takes the place of the kitchen sink window in this enclosed kitchen, though it is hardly the focal point. Designer Susan Seals drew the eye to the cabinets, with classic relief work and floral wallpaper and ceiling border. Granite countertop and back splashes provide easy maintenance.

Left: Allen Godziebiewski designed this incredible glass-front cabinet and the complementing rounded cabinets for this enclosed kitchen. White and black create a modern look, with lighting inset in cabinet overhangs.

Below: Wood was designer Anda Schmaltz's medium of choice in this kitchen dominated by paneled ceiling, heavy beams, and expansive cabinets. The counter wraps around like a donut shop, and these comfortable-looking chairs are, no doubt, rarely unoccupied.

Photos courtesy of NKBA

Natural elements harmonize in this kitchen designed by David Lemkin. Natural wood, copper range hood, and faux marble floor lend warmth to the cabinet surrounded space, with a cook's island and a sink area with raised table for seating.

Left: Natural wood and artful curves lend elegant simplicity to this kitchen designed by Diana Valentine.
Photo courtesy of NKBA

Below: White makes this kitchen space sparkle, extending into a dining area. A few black touches—chairs, refrigerator exhaust, and check pattern in the floor tiles—stand out in marked contrast in this design by Joyce Wyman.
Photo by Carol Bates/Courtesy of NKBA

An attached table is a highlight of this black and white kitchen. A rich wood floor and frosted-glass lighting fixtures add elegance to the overall design by Michael Palkowitschm.

This is a kitchen ready for business—with double ovens, double-wide, side-by-side refrigerator, and a stainless steel range and hood. Yet designer Thomas D. Kling has softened the overall effect with lots of wood, terra-cotta tiles, and country accents including a fanciful hanging fixture over the island for displaying copper pots and wicker baskets.

A sunny tile back splash behind the stove plus delicate
window treatment and hanging lights add elegance to this
traditional, natural-wood kitchen designed by Alan Asarnow.

A picture window gets maximum play in this small kitchen designed by Donna H. Snover. A counter that curves out beside the stove and rangetop adds additional work space, as well as seating.

Left: The instruments of cooking make simple adornments in this kitchen designed by Patti A. Kronour. A row of hanging pots and pans above the industrial-size cook range draw the eye, and windows to the outdoors provide visual relief for the slave to the stove.

Below: Designer Tom Trzcinski had lots of space to work with in this kitchen design, and he maximized it. The focal point is the copper-topped fireplace that ties dining and food preparation areas together. Zones have been established for cooking, and there is a wet bar for serving drinks, connected via a window and continuous countertop to the dining area.

Photo by Walter Smalling, Jr./Courtesy of NKBA

Photo by Wayne Simco/Courtesy of NKBA

Open-face cabinets, a glass table with cast-iron chairs, and an Oriental carpet take this kitchen into another realm of the home in this design by Shirley J. McFarlane. Food preparation areas connect directly with more casual, comfortable parts of the home.

Molded accents on the cabinetry give this kitchen by Sandra L.
Steiner-Houck and Marianne Heidelbaugh its classic charm.
The arched doorway and modern fireplace update the effect.

A painted tile scene dominates this room, framed by open-faced cabinets. An enormous island dominates the kitchen, which was designed by Barton Lindsky.

An industrial stove is nestled amidst custom tile work, topped by a wood framed hood and display area in a design by Joan E. Zimmerman and Mary Bland. This kitchen's utilitarian, country charm is also enhanced by antique-finished wood cabinetry, a double-Dutch door, and an old-fashioned butcher block.

A modern look is created using opaque glass and a raw wood finish, contrasted with dark stone floor. A high ceiling, open beams, and enormous windows add to the airy feel created by enormous expanses of cabinetry and counter. Lovely blue emphasis was added with suspended lighting in this design by Connie L. Gustafson.

Resource Guide

Andersen Windows, Inc.
100 Fourth Avenue, North
Bayport, MN 55003-1096
Phone: 800-426-4261, ext. 2826
www.andersenwindows.com

Alan Asarnow, CKD, CBD
Ulrich, Inc.
Ridgewood, NJ

Ann Sacks Tile and Stone, Inc.
8120 NE 33rd Drive
Portland, Oregon 97211
Phone: 503-281-7751
www.annsackstile.com

Joyce Bishop, CKD
Cutters Kitchen & Bath
Des Peres, MO

Mary Bland
Design Solutions
Annapolis, MD

Bomanite Corporation
P.O. Box 599
Madera, CA 93639-0599
Phone: 209-673-2411
Fax: 209-673-8246
bomanite@bomanite.com
www.bomanite.com

Bruce© Hardwood Floors
16803 Dallas Parkway
Dallas, TX 75248
Phone: 214-931-3100

Pamela Brunderman
Interior Designer
Seven Lake Street, 8J
White Plains, NY 10603
Phone: 914-421-0573

Jack L. Busby
Design Cabinets & Furniture, Inc.
Alachua, FL

Jean Cain
Comprehensive Design
1219 Silverado Trail
Napa, CA 94559
Phone: 707-252-0709

Canac Kitchens Ltd.
360 John Street
Thornhill, Ontario L3T 3M9
Phone: 905-881-2153
www.canackitchens.com

Congoleum Corp.
P.O. Box 8116
Trenton, NJ 08650-0116
Phone: 800-934-3567
www.congoleum.com

DuPont Corian©
Barley Mill Plaza/Price Mill Building
P.O. Box 80012
Wilmington, DE 19880-0012
Phone: 800-426-7426
Fax: 302-992-2882
www.corian.com

Crossville Porcelain Stone
P.O. Box 1168
Crossville, TN 38557
Phone: 931-484-2110
Fax: 931-484-8418
cross@crossville.com
www.crossville-ceramics.com

Annette M. DePaepe, CKD, CBD
AMD Designs
Hackettstown, NJ

Joan DesCombes, CKD
Architectural Artworks, Inc.
Winter Park, FL

Catherine A. Dulacki, CKD
WM OHS Showrooms, Inc.
Denver, CO

Beverly Ellsley
Interior Design
Westport, CT

Elmira Stove Works
595 Colby Drive
Waterloo, Ontario
N2V 1A2
Phone: 519-725-5500
Fax: 519-725-5503
www.elmirastoveworks.com

Allen Godziebiewski
Cabinets by Robert
Traverse City, MI

Connie L. Gustafson, CKD
Sawhill Custom Kitchens and Design,
Inc.
Minneapolis, MN

IXL Cabinets
16803 Dallas Parkway
Dallas, TX 75248
Phone: 214-887-2483
Fax: 214-887-2434

Karen R. Edwards, CKD, CBD
Karen Edwards Design
Watkins Glen, NY

Merrie Fredericks, CKD, CBD
Design Concepts Plus
Havertown, PA

The Hardwood Council
P.O. Box 525
Oakmont, PA 15139
Phone: 412-281-2980
www.hardwoodcouncil.com

Barbara Hauben-Ross
Interior Design
New York, NY

HDM USA
Natural Impressions™
4200 Northside Parkway
Building 4, Suite 100
Atlanta, GA 30327
Phone: 404-842-0777

Marianne Heidelbaugh
Columbia, PA

Delores L. Hyden
The Showplace, Inc.
Redmond, WA

Candace Ihlenfeldt, CKD
Carmel Valley, CA

Jenn-Air
403 West Forth St.
Newton, IA 50208
Phone: 800-536-6247
www.jennair.com

Gary S. Johnson
International Kitchen & Bath Ex-
change
Sunnyvale, CA

Dena Rae Jurries, CKD
Dena Jurries Kitchen & Bath Design
Boise, ID

The Kennebec Company
Designers & Cabinetmakers
One Front Street
Bath, Maine 04530
Phone: 207-443-2131
Fax: 207-443-4380
www.kennebec@gwi.net

Thomas Kling, CKD
Thomas D. Kling, Inc.
York, PA

Molly J. Korb, CKD, CBD
MK Designs
Newcastle, CA

Patti A. Kronour, CKD
Pasco Design & Consulting
Middletown, OH

Kohler Co.
Kohler, WI 53044
Phone: 920-457-444
800-454-6537
www.kohlerco.com

Jason Landau
Kitchen Works
Hewlett, NY

Ted Langenfield
Architect/Interior Design
Nebraska Custom Kitchens
4061 Dodge Street
Omaha, NE 68132
Phone: 402-561-1000

Susan M. Larsen, CKD, CBD
Bolig Kitchen Studio
Woodinville, VA

Legendary Hardwood Floors
601 South 21st Street
Terre Haute, IN 47803
Phone: 812-232-3372
Fax: 812-234-6794

David Lemkin, CKD
Kitchen Specialists of California
Encino, CA

Daniel J. Lenner, CKD, CBD
Morris Black & Sons, Inc.
Allentown, PA

Shirley J. McFarlane, CKD
Kitchensmith Inc.
Atlanta, GA

Merillat Industries Inc.
P.O. Box 1946
Adrian, MI 49221
Phone: 517-263-0771

Maureen O'Brien-Morsch, CKD, CBD
Home Systems
Lafayette, CA

Michael Palkowitsch, CKD, CBD
Michael Palkowitsch Design
St. Paul, MN

Kelly L. Peterson
WM OHS Showrooms, Inc.
Denver, CO

Pergo
524 New Hope Road
Raleigh, NC 27610
Phone: 800-337-3746
www.pergo.com

Plain & Fancy Custom Cabinetry
Box 519
Schaefferstown, PA 17088
Phone: 717-949-6571

Karen Richmond, CKD, CBD
Neil Kelly Designers/Remodelers
Portland, OR

Rutt Custom Cabinetry, LLC
1564 Main Street
Goodville, PA 17528
717-445-3708
www. Rutt1.com

Matha Sasso & S. J. Pappas
Meriden, CT

Anda Schmaltz, CKD, CBD
Hyland Bros. Lumber
Lincoln, NE

Susan Seals
Award Winning Interiors, Inc.
Morristown, TN

Sears
Phone: 800-359-2000
www.commercial.sears.com

Shanker Industries
3435 Lawson Blvd.
Oceanside, N.Y. 11572
Phone: 516-766-4477
Fax: 516-766-6655

The Sherwin-Williams Co.
Phone: 800-336-1110, ext. 1097

Diane H. Small, CKD
Diane H. Small, Inc.
McLean, VA

Donna H. Snover, CKD, CBD
Morris Black & Sons
Allentown, PA

Southern Pine Council
P.O. Box 641700
Kenner, LA 70064-1700
Phone: 504-443-4464
Fax: 504-443-6612
mail@sfpa.org
www.southernpine.com

Sandra L. Steiner-Houch, CKD
Columbia, PA

Thermador®
5551 McFadden Avenue
Huntington, Beach, CA 92649
Phone: 800-656-9226

Tom Trzcinski, CKD, CBD
Kitchen & Bath Concepts of Pittsburgh
Pittsburgh, PA

Whirlpool Corp.
2000 M-63
Benton Harbor, MI 49022-2692
Phone: 616-923-7200

Robert Wieland, CKD, CBD
Kitchens by Wieland
Allentown, PA

Wilsonart Laminate Flooring
2400 Wilson Place
Temple, TX 76503
Phone: 254-207-7000
www.wilsonart.com

Wellborne Cabinet, Inc.
38669 Highway 77
P.O. Box 1210
Ashland, AL 36251
Phone: 265-354-7151
Fax: 265-354-7022
www.wellborncabinet.com

Wood-Mode Fine Custom Cabinetry
One Second Street
Kreamer, PA 17833
717-374-2711

Joyce Wyman, CKD
Pompanette Kitchens
West Palm Beach, FL

Diana Valentine, CKD, CBD
Showplace Kitchen & Bath.
Redmond, WA

Yorktowne Cabinets
P.O. Box 231
Red Lion, PA 17356-0231
Phone: 717-244-4011

Joan E. Zimmerman, CKD, CBD
Design Solutions
Annapolis, MD